T0260062

Macintosh Troubleshooting
Pocket Guide

David Lerner and Aaron Freimark,
Tekserve Corporation

O'REILLY®

Beijing · Boston · Farnham · Sebastopol · Tokyo

Macintosh Troubleshooting Pocket Guide
by David Lerner and Aaron Freimark

Copyright © 2003 David Lerner. All rights reserved. Printed in the United States of America.

Published by O'Reilly & Associates, Inc., 1005 Gravenstein Highway North, Sebastopol, CA 95472.

O'Reilly & Associates books may be purchased for educational, business, or sales promotional use. Online editions are also available for most titles (*safari.oreilly.com*). For more information, contact our corporate/institutional sales department: (800) 998-9938 or *corporate@oreilly.com*.

Editors:	Tim O'Reilly and Nancy Kotary
Production Editor:	Darren Kelly
Cover Designer:	Emma Colby
Interior Designer:	David Futato

Printing History:

November 2002:	First Edition

978-0-596-00443-9
[LSI]

Contents

Foreword

A few months ago, I read a story in the New York Times about Tekserve, an iconoclastic Mac-only repair shop in Manhattan. I approached David Lerner, one of the founders, about writing a Mac hardware book for us. No time, he said. But he mentioned that he'd written an FAQ (Frequently Asked Questions) document that Tekserve gives out to its customers and makes available for download on its web site.

It's not the *Mac Hardware in a Nutshell* that I was hoping for, but it's a pretty darn useful document for any Mac user out there, and I thought it was worth sharing with Mac users who don't happen to live in New York City or its environs, so I asked David if I could publish it as a little pocket guide.

Fortunately, he was willing to entertain the notion. I hope you enjoy Tekserve's advice as much as I have.

—Tim O'Reilly

Macintosh Troubleshooting Pocket Guide

Introduction

Macintosh computers work quite smoothly. And Mac users find them relatively easy to use. However, on some occasion, your Mac might need a repair, or you might need help figuring out how to troubleshoot a problem with Mac hardware or software.

This book is useful in these types of situations. We hope it will save you an unnecessary trip or tech-support call. In this guide, we give you the technician's answers to frequently asked questions. We also let you know which problems are serious enough to require help from an expert.

This book is essentially a list of common questions and answers. It's short enough that you can read through it and discover some useful new tricks, but it's also organized by topic, so that you can flip to the section you need in an emergency. And it's small enough that you can throw it in your computer bag if you're using a laptop.

We cover the following topics:

- Avoiding the technician or consultant
- Being prepared
- Crisis situations
- Bombs and crashes
- The System (OS 9.x and earlier)

- Mac OS X (including passwords and multiple users)
- Printers
- Connecting older devices to newer Macs
- SCSI, FireWire, and USB devices
- Monitors/displays
- Memory
- Viruses
- Powerbooks and iBooks
- Communications, the Internet, and AirPort
- File sharing

There's also a section on other questions that don't fall into these categories.

We indicate tips that apply to Mac OS 9 and Mac OS X by including [9] and [X], respectively, at the end of the section or question.

We cover the most popular questions from new and experienced Mac users, but you might have one to add to future versions of this guide. If you think the answer to your question might be useful to other Mac users, please send your suggestion to: *book@tekserve.com*

Avoid Going to Your Technician or Consultant in a Panic

Your dealer, repair technician, or consultant is there to help. But wouldn't it be nice to be able to take care of some things on your own? Here are some basic steps that will allow you to handle some emergencies yourself:

1. Save multiple copies of critical files on multiple drives, disks, or tapes. In short, backup constantly and religiously, especially when you are under deadline pressure. Save early and often. When you are working on

important documents, you may want to periodically save a new version (append a letter to the name, like *important work a*, *important work b*).

2. Don't save the only version of an important file on a floppy, Zip, or CD (in fact, you should never have only one copy of an important file). Make multiple copies. Don't erase your last backup to make a new one—you might be backing up a corrupted file and might need the previous backup.

3. At least one of your recent backups should be in a different location (i.e., off-site). When working on critical material, you can email a copy to a co-worker or another email account once in a while. An Apple .Mac (dotmac) account for $99 per year includes 100 MB of off-site storage on Apple's servers via a very simple backup program that can perform scheduled backups.

4. Install and use the latest version of your preferred anti-viral software (such as Virex—part of Apple's .Mac—or Norton AntiVirus). You should be sure to install the monthly anti-virus updates, which is normally as simple as clicking on an "Update" button in the program.

5. Run the latest Apple Disk First Aid (this is part of Disk Utility in Mac OS X) on your drives once a month or so (always backup first). After a full backup, you can also safely use DiskWarrior, TechTool, Norton or Drive 10. Of these, DiskWarrior is our favorite, and Tech Tool is for OS 9 only.

6. If you own a current version of Norton Utilities (7.0.2 was current as of October 2002), enable FileSaver (but please disable Crashguard).

7. Own the software you use, read the manuals, and keep the original program CDs in a safe place. You might also want to back up copies of important application installer CDs and keep them off-site.

Being Prepared

Spend a little time getting ready to cope with a problem before you have one. All recent Macs come with a bootable CD-ROM with System software—keep it handy. If you own a copy of Norton Disk Doctor or DiskWarrior, keep it up to date and be sure that it will boot your CPU. It's also helpful in many recovery situations to have an external storage device like a FireWire hard drive. It's even better if you install a bootable system on that drive.

My hard drive has trouble getting going, but it always starts after a few tries. Should I bother backing it up?

No, your data is of no importance and you can probably recreate it within a few months. After all, you have lots of paper printouts to recopy from and you're a fast typist.

Seriously, if your computer or hard drive is doing anything unusual—squeaking, chirping, having trouble getting going, read/write errors, missing or damaged files—take it as a reminder to do a complete backup to another drive, removable media, or over the Web. Please!

How do I know what version of the System software I have?

Click on your desktop. Then click in the Apple menu at the top-left corner of your screen. The first item will say "About this Mac" or "About this Macintosh" or "About this Computer." Inside there will be the version of your System: 7.1 or 8.5.1 or 9.2 or 10.2.1 or something like that. This window also tells you how much (built-in) memory you have.

How do I know what Mac I'm using? [9 & X]

If the Mac is vintage 1997 or earlier, the model name is printed on the front or top of the case (PowerMac 6100, PowerBook Duo 230, Quadra 630, SE/30, etc.). Make sure you are looking at the computer case and not the monitor case.

In 1997, Apple began the unfortunate practice of using the same designation for computers even after many internal and external modifications. There are nine models of iMac, for example, each with different capabilities. Apple has official parenthetical names, like iMac (Slot-Loading CD-ROM), but you won't find these on the computer case. The AppleSpec database at *http://www.info.apple.com/support/applespec.html* lists the official names and dates of production for all Macs.

If you have Mac OS X 10.2 or later, open the Apple Menu, choose "About this Mac," and click on the More Info button. The Hardware Overview may tell you the exact machine model (for example, "Power Mac G4 [AGP graphics]"), the machine speed, and the number of processors. If it's not so specific, keep reading.

If you have Mac OS X 10.0 or 10.1, you can find Apple System Profiler inside your *Applications/Utilities* folder. If you are using Mac OS 9.x or earlier, it's inside the Apple Menu. These earlier versions won't tell you the exact machine model (only Power Mac G4), but it will tell you the speed and number of processors, which are often enough clues to find your model in the AppleSpec database.

You may be able to determine your Mac's date of production from its serial number. You can find the serial number in the Apple System Profiler, or on the back or bottom of the case. PowerBooks have their serial number inside the battery compartment, and iBooks have it underneath the keyboard. The third character of the serial number is your Mac's year of production (9=1999, 1=2001, etc.), and the fourth and fifth characters are the week of that year, from 01 to 52. So a serial number of SG951643-HP0 tells me it was born at the end of December, 1999.

PowerBook G3 physical identification:

• PowerBookG3 "Kanga," introduced 10/97, 250MHz, looks like PowerBook 3400c, has speaker vents on top case and Apple logo in Color, has HDI-30 SCSI port, family M3553.

- PowerBook G3 "Wall Street," introduced 5/98, 233, 250 or 292 MHz (266 and 300 MHz introduced 5/99), has black keyboard, solid white Apple logo and mini-din Serial port, and HDI-30 SCSI port, family M4753.
- PowerBook G3 Bronze Keyboard "Lombard," introduced 5/99, 333 or 400 MHz, has bronze keyboard, solid white Apple logo and USB Ports (but no FireWire), family M5343.
- PowerBook G3 FireWire introduced 2/00, 400 or 500 MHz, has bronze keyboard, solid white Apple logo, USB Ports and FireWire ports, family M7572.

PowerBook G4 physical identification:

- PowerBook G4 Titanium, introduced 2/01, 400 or 500 MHz, has DB-15 VGA connector, solid back door without slots. Bottom case has Phillips (cross-head) screws.
- PowerBook G4 Titanium (Gigabit Ethernet), introduced 11/01, 550 or 667 MHz, has DB-15 VGA connector, back door has vertical vent slots. Bottom case has Torx screws.
- PowerBook G4 Titanium DVI, introduced 4/02, 667 or 800 MHz, has DVI video connector on back panel, back door has vertical vent slots. Bottom case has Torx screws.

Power Macintosh G4 Tower physical identification:

- Power Macintosh G4 (PCI Graphics) VGA video, sound ports in middle of rear panel aligned horizontally, has Plaintalk mic/line input jack, lacks internal AirPort slot, has power outlet jack for a monitor, 350 or 400 MHz, Model M7631 or M7826.
- Power Macintosh G4 (AGP Graphics) VGA or VGA & DVI video, sound ports in middle of rear panel aligned vertically, has Plaintalk mic/line input jack, has power outlet jack for a monitor, 350, 400, 450 MHz, Model M6921, M7232, M7824, M7825, M7827.

- Power Macintosh G4 (Gigabit Ethernet), VGA and ADC video, sound ports in middle of rear panel aligned vertically, has power outlet jack for a monitor, 400, 450 Dual or 500 MHz, Model M7891, M7892 or M7893.

- Power Macintosh G4 (Digital Audio), VGA and ADC video, sound ports at top of rear panel aligned vertically, 466, 533, Dual 533, 667 or 733 MHz, M7627, M7688, M7945, or M7681.

- Power Macintosh G4 (Quicksilver) VGA and ADC video, front panel has two oval-ended drive doors, 733, Dual 800 or 867 MHz, Model M8359, M8360, or M8361.

- Power Macintosh G4 (Quicksilver 2002), VGA and ADC video (dual display capable), front panel has two oval-ended drive doors, 800, 933 MHz or Dual 1 Ghz, Model M8705, M8666, M8667.

- Power Macintosh G4 (Mirrored Drive Door) DVI and ADC video (dual display–capable), front panel has "mirrored" drive doors, Dual 867 MHz, Dual 1 GHz and Dual 1.25 GHz, Model M8787, M8689, M8573.

For help identifying your iMac model, check out the Apple Knowledge Base article at *http://www.info.apple.com/kbnum/ n58669.*

Crisis Situations

I turned on my computer and just see a little blinking picture of a floppy disk, system folder, or a question mark. [9 & X]

Try starting from the System Install CD-ROM that came with your computer. If the CD or disk is ejected, you may have a stuck button on your mouse or trackball. Or perhaps it isn't really a startup disk and is lacking the software needed to boot your computer. Turn off the Mac, unplug the mouse or trackball, and then see if it starts okay from the CD or your hard disk. If so, the mouse or trackball is the culprit.

What you do next depends on your system version.

WARNING

In some instances, repair programs will make things worse. This is why we say to always back up everything, so that, if a repair fails, you have another recourse.

If you have OS 9 or earlier:

1. If it starts up okay from your System CD and you see your hard disk icon below the CD icon, the System on your hard drive may have become damaged. If so, back up your important files, run Disk First Aid to repair any directory damage, and then reinstall the System. If that doesn't solve the problem, try a "clean System install," which is described later in this book.

2. If your hard disk drive icon doesn't show up under the CD or floppy icon, you can try running Disk First Aid. If Disk First Aid sees your hard drive, it may be able to fix problems in the directory. If it finds things to fix, run it again to be sure that everything is really fixed. If it keeps saying it fixed the same thing each time you run it, it's lying to you.

3. If you own Norton Utilities, Tech Tool Pro, or Disk-Warrior, you can try them now (but please read the next question first).

If you have Mac OS X:

1. Insert your Mac OS X Install disk, and wait until the Installer finishes loading.

2. At the first Installer screen, look under the "Installer" menu, and choose "Open Disk Utility...."

3. If you see your disk(s) on the left side of the Disk Utility window, you can try to repair it using Disk Utility. Open the triangles to see the name of each volume on your Mac. Choose your startup volume, click the "First Aid" tab, and then click "Repair." When finished, quit Disk Utility, quit the Installer *without* installing, and restart. If

you get a blinking system folder, you might need to reinstall your system.

4. If your hard disk or volume didn't show up in Disk Utility, you can try using Norton Utilities, Tech Tool Pro, or DiskWarrior, even if your version is not Mac OS X–native. However, make sure it is no more than a year old, and please read the next question first.

Can I make things worse by doing repairs with Norton Disk Doctor, Tech Tool, DiskWarrior, or Disk First Aid? [9 & X]

Unfortunately, yes. In most instances, these programs are good tools that help solve problems. But "repairing" certain problems can leave you worse off than before—in some cases, even destroy a disk from which a professional could easily have recovered data to a complete loss situation. Basically, when your drive's directory is scrambled, anything that writes to the disk has the potential to do harm. Running Norton Disk Doctor or Tech Tool Pro actually writes to the directory that it's fixing, so occasionally it does damage. However, running a data recovery utility such as Data Rescue, Norton's Volume Recover, or Unerase should be fine, if you copy the recovered files to a different drive. If you recover the files onto the damaged drive, you will be overwriting other data you wish to recover, compounding existing directory damage, and making things worse. The latest Norton Utilities offers to save an "undo" file so that you can go backwards, but we've had Norton crash in the middle of a repair, and the Undo file itself was corrupted or incomplete.

You can also use DiskWarrior to recreate a disk directory, but don't rush to write the new directory to the disk. Instead, click the "preview" button on DiskWarrior's last screen to mount the volume using the rebuilt directory and back up your files to another drive. Check the files thoroughly before you write the new directory or reformat the old drive.

If you are well backed up, you can use any repair utility with confidence. If you are not backed up and your data is essential to you, consider getting professional help. We're not trying to scare you into always hiring us—we're trying to scare you into always making lots of backups!

Word just crashed, and I hadn't saved. Can I get back my work? [9 & X]

If you have OS 9 and earlier, before you restart the computer, search for "Word Temp" or "Word Work" files and move them to the desktop. They may contain some saved work.

If you have Mac OS X: Word X is a little smarter and will usually show your last unsaved work when you launch the program after a crash, but it may not be complete, which is why you want to save regularly.

NOTE

Chow-hound Jim Leff (*http://www.chowhound.com*) says: "Search & Rescue is a program that floats under most Mac-users' radar, but it's absolutely invaluable. It recovers *unsaved* text. If a word processor, email app, etc., crashes and you'd neglected to save the text you were working on, Search & Rescue recovers all your work. Rarely fails, works like magic for any application, even re-covers unsaved text after a restart(!). It has saved my ass many, many, many times. Just $15 shareware. I'm a fan and beta tester (and the author quotes me on his site), but I have no financial interest and don't know the guy personally." You can find it at *http://www.versiontracker.com* if you search for "search rescue" (Mac OS 9 only).

My keyboard doesn't work, and I get little beeps when I press a key. [9 & X]

You have probably accidentally enabled Easy Access, a special Apple control panel to help disabled people use the Mac keyboard. If you're working on OS 9 and earlier, open the Easy Access control panel and turn off each of its features. If you're working on OS X, open Universal Access in System Preferences and turn off sticky keys.

I turn on my computer and hear a series of musical notes or beeps (or what sounds like a car crash or broken glass), or I get a picture of an unhappy Mac on the screen with some numbers under it. [9 & X]

This can happen if you have certain older CD-ROMs in your drive when you boot, so first try removing any CD-ROMs. If that doesn't cure it, read on.

Every time you start your Mac, it does some diagnostics on itself. With these signals, the Mac is telling you that those diagnostics failed.

1. Turn everything off, and disconnect all external SCSI, USB, and FireWire devices (except your mouse and keyboard). These are things such as scanners, hard drives, Zip, printers, and so on. Now that your external stuff is disconnected, start the Mac and see if the problem was caused by the external devices. If so, reconnect them one at a time to see when the problem returns. With SCSI, you must turn everything off before connecting or disconnecting devices.

2. Zap the PRAM. This is special *parameter memory* that stores crucial settings for your Mac and can become corrupted. Zapping it means resetting it to the original defaults. On newer Macs, hold down ⌘-Option-P-R while turning on the Mac. Keep holding those keys down until you hear the startup bong two or three times. (On the PowerBook 190, 1400, 2300, 2400, 3400, and 5300, when you have successfully zapped the PRAM, the screen may be blank and the green sleep LED may be steadily lit—you then need to press the reset button on the rear of the computer.) If this doesn't work, continue with the next step.

3. A series of beeps on recent Macs can indicate a hardware problem, usually bad or incompatible RAM. On some machines, the power LED will flash as many times as the

beeps, plus one, repeating the sequence every five seconds. Apple sometimes changes the definitions of beeps on new machines, so you may want to check the online Apple Knowledgebase (*http://kbase.info.apple.com*) for your specific machine. The current beep codes are:

- 1 beep = all RAM sockets are empty
- 2 beeps = incompatible RAM installed
- 3 beeps = RAM failed test
- 4 beeps = problem with the boot ROM on the logic board
- 5 beeps = processor is bad

4. On recent Macs, restart holding down the Option key to bring up the startup manager. On older Macs, restart by holding down ⌘-Shift-Option-Delete. You have to hold down all four buttons together, and then, while keeping those buttons down, turn on the computer. This tells the computer to ignore the normal startup drive. If instead of the sad tones or sad Mac you now get a blinking picture of a disk or folder, then your disk driver (or the System file) is probably corrupted. The disk driver is special information on your hard drive that tells the Mac how to talk to the hard drive.

We're getting into dangerous territory if you aren't backed up. If you are backed up, or not concerned about anything on your hard drive, try restarting from a System CD-ROM or Disk Tools floppy while holding down those four buttons (or with the Option key). If this works, under OS 9.x or earlier, run Apple Drive Setup and select "Update driver" from the Functions selection.

WARNING

Don't click "Initialize"—that will wipe out everything on your drive. If you have used a driver-level compression program such as eDisk, Times Two, or Stacker, even updating the driver can wipe out your data.

Under Mac OS X, boot from your system CD, launch Disk Utility, click the First Aid tab, click the reveal triangle on your hard drive (if it shows up), highlight your volume name, and click the Repair button.

If you recently added RAM to the computer, you may want to try removing it (if you are comfortable doing this and have the right anti-static equipment).

5. If you still get the sad Mac tones, your problems are more serious—either memory, the motherboard, the hard drive, or an add-on such as an accelerator, nuBus, or PCI card. At this point, if you still have trouble, you should probably bring the computer in for service.

My trackpad is jumping around.

Brushing a second finger against the trackpad can cause this, but trackpads respond to the capacitance of your finger and are affected by moisture. Try washing and drying your hands.

My mouse and keyboard stopped working.

Try unplugging and replugging the mouse. If this doesn't help, turn off the computer, and try plugging only the mouse into the back of the computer and restarting. If this works, your computer itself is okay, but there is probably a bad connection in the jack in your keyboard. Try a replacement keyboard.

NOTE

Recent Macs and iMacs have USB ports, and it is fine to plug in USB devices (and FireWire devices) when the computer is on. USB devices have square or rectangular plugs and sockets. Older Macs use ADB ports with a round four-pin plug and socket, and those can be damaged by hot-plugging devices.

My Mac froze up. Now what? [9 & X]

First check for simple stuff, like the mouse connector came loose from the keyboard. Sometimes just unplugging and replugging the mouse will cause the Mac to "wake up."

If you have unsaved work, there is a very slim chance of rescuing it. ⌘-Option-Escape will let you force-quit the current program (the one that froze).

In OS 9 and earlier, you might be able to get to any other programs and save your work in them before quitting and restarting. But you will lose what you've done in the current program. When you restart, move the "rescued items" folder out of the trash (if there is one). It might contain temporary files used by your crashed program, and part of your unsaved work might be there.

In Mac OS X, force-quitting a native program does not affect other programs, and you won't need to restart. Force-quitting a Classic program may or may not bring down other Classic programs; follow the guidelines for OS 9.

If these suggestions don't work, you've probably lost all your work since you last saved. Restart with the power switch or the reset button or press these three buttons together: ⌘-Control-Power on (on Macs without a reset button). After restarting, you can try to recover lost text with the shareware Search & Rescue, as mentioned earlier.

A disk is stuck in my Mac.

Don't pull it out with pliers; that might destroy the drive. Try launching iTunes and clicking the Eject button in the lower right corner. If this doesn't work, try restarting the computer while holding down the mouse button. If this doesn't work, try ejecting the disk by pushing a straightened paper clip into the little hole alongside the drive. If this doesn't work, the Mac probably needs to be disassembled to get the disk out, and the drive might even be damaged. If your Mac has a slot-loading CD or DVD drive, you should insert only regular round 5.25" discs. Minidiscs and novelty CDs (like business-card-shaped discs) will get stuck, and might even void your warranty.

I just spilled beer/tea/cough syrup on my keyboard (well, my cat threw up on it).

Shut down, unplug the keyboard from the computer, and turn it upside down. Wait a day or few for it to dry. It may all be okay now. If not, buy a new keyboard. (Former *Byte* columnist Jerry Pournelle says just to take it in the shower with you and rinse it thoroughly and then dry it for a few days, but he also believes in Star Wars missile defenses.) If it's an iBook or a PowerBook, remove the battery and the power cord and bring it in for service immediately. Don't turn it on! The internal backup battery can cause electrolytic corrosion and lead to an expensive logic board repair. Damage caused by spills is *not* covered by warranty or AppleCare (but may be covered by some insurance policies).

Every five to thirty minutes my computer slows down to a crawl and there is a lot of disk activity. What's wrong? [9]

It could be the Autostart worm virus. See "Viruses" later in this book. With Mac OS 8.6, it could also be a problem with DHCP (involved in TCP/IP networking and used to access some networks or DSL/cable modems); updating to Mac OS 9.0 or higher should solve the problem.

My computer takes several minutes to boot. [9]

Your computer may be looking for a server that is no longer available. Try moving the "Servers" folder from your System Folder to the desktop and restarting. If this fixes it, you can throw away the Servers folder; if not, put it back.

I recently upgraded to OS X 10.2 (Jaguar) on my iMac DV and now have no video. [X]

If your Mac had OS 8.6 and you installed Jaguar, you might not have installed the Firmware Update 4.1.9 (or later) that comes with OS 9.2. You need to boot the iMac with an external monitor, install 9.2, and run the iMac Firmware Updater.

Bombs and Crashes

My computer bombs whenever I launch my MajorSoft WordMangler program. [9]

If your problems occur only with one particular program or action, and are fairly repeatable, they should be easy to fix:

1. Try giving the program more memory. Be sure the program is not running, then click once on the icon of the program and press ⌘-I (Get Info). On newer systems, choose "Show: Memory" from the pop-up list. Increase the "preferred" memory size by 25–100% and try the program again.

2. Check the vendor's web site or *http://www. versiontracker.com* for updates or patches to the program, and try installing them. You may have a known problem that has already been solved.

3. Try starting without extensions. The vendor will tell you to do this, so try it first. Hold down the Shift key while the Mac starts up. It should say "Welcome to Macintosh (or Mac OS), Extensions disabled." If the problem is gone, see the next question and answer entry.

4. Quit the program, and then delete any preferences files used by the program. If they are complicated preferences, copy them to another folder or a disk in case it turns out they're not the problem and you want to restore them. The preferences file is usually in the Preferences folder in the System Folder, but it could be somewhere else, such as in the folder with the program (or in the "Claris" or "Aldus" or "your software brand name here" folder). Then reinstall the program from the original disk or CD and run any updaters.

5. Some problems can be traced to corrupted, damaged or compressed fonts. Try removing the Fonts folder from your System Folder. If you are using Suitcase, ATM Deluxe, or MasterJuggler, also use it to close all your fonts. Restart the computer, and see if the problem is solved. If so, you need to work your way through your fonts and see which one is the culprit. A corrupted ATM cache file or ATM database can also cause grief, but you can safely delete them.

6. If it's Office 98 (Word, Excel, or PowerPoint) that's causing problems or complaining about DLLs or Visual Basic, delete the "Office Registration Cache" and "PPC Registration Database" preference files.

7. If these steps don't solve the problem, contact the company that publishes the program. Many vendors offer good free tech support, and sometimes you will have a standard problem that they can quickly identify and tell you how to fix. Many vendors also have support forums online. This is especially useful for those vendors that charge for telephone tech support, as their online support is still free. You also get the benefit of the input from other users, who may have encountered the same problems and have workarounds you can use until the vendor fixes the bug. Some companies also have decent support on their web site.

Every time I restart my Mac, I get a bomb just after the Finder loads. What now? [9]

You might have a corrupted print file. Restart with the shift key down to disable extensions. Then open the desktop printer icon (it will have a big X through it) and trash whatever files you find inside it.

All my icons are generic with folded corners. Where are the regular icons? [9]

Your hidden "Desktop" files are damaged or corrupted. See the next question.

I double-clicked on a file and the computer said, "the application that created it cannot be found." Will rebuilding the desktop help? [9]

The invisible "Desktop" file(s) keep track of the icon for each file and which applications are used to open that file. If the desktop file gets corrupted, these problems occur, and the answer is to rebuild the desktop. Restart your computer and press ⌘-Option. When you see a message saying "Are you sure you want to rebuild the desktop?", click Yes.

Of course, some files aren't meant to be opened directly and should give that error message. And sometimes you really don't have the required application. The shareware Graphic-Converter program is a gem—it can open, edit, print, and save graphics files in any of more than a dozen formats, and costs only $35. MacLink Plus is the top general-purpose translator program and supports many text, word-processing, spreadsheet, and database file types.

My computer bombs when I turn it on. [9]

Many bombs can be traced to extensions and control panels that modify system behavior (and sometimes each other's behavior). Under System 7 and up, holding down the Shift key while booting will disable all of them. If this solves the problem, use Extensions Manager to disable specific control panels and extensions. The usual suggestion is to try turning off half your extensions; if the problem doesn't go away, try the other half. When you find the half that causes the problem, disable half of that, and so on, until you isolate the problem.

There are commercial programs like Conflict Catcher that automate extension troubleshooting.

If disabling extensions doesn't solve the problem, it may be a hardware or system problem. Try booting from a System Install or Restore CD. If this solves things, try a clean System install (see the next section).

The System (OS 9.x and Earlier)

What's the big deal about the System Folder? [9]

System software is what makes your Mac smile when you turn it on, allows it to run, read and write hard drives, copy files, run other programs, and all sorts of other goodies. The Finder is part of the System software and is usually the program that runs first when the computer starts up. The System software lives in a folder that is usually named "System Folder," which contains the critical files "System" and "Finder," as well as many related files. In System 7 and newer versions, these related files are mostly in folders in the System Folder, such as *Extensions, Control Panels, Preferences*, and in 7.1 and up, *Fonts*.

If everyone just used the System Folder the way it comes from Apple, there would be far fewer crashes, bombs, and conflicts. But many programs add files or even folders to the System Folder, and most of us have added various system enhancements (anti-virus programs, security programs, and font management programs, such as Suitcase, FileSaver, and so on).

When your system is operating flawlessly, make a backup of your System Folder. It's easiest to do this with a backup program like Retrospect. Or you can boot from a CD or another drive, and then copy your System Folder to another disk or removable media, or use Apple's Disk Copy to save a "disk image" of the entire System Folder. If you have trouble later, you can restore that backup and get back to work. If you do this, save the messed-up System Folder by renaming the folder and dragging its Finder to the trash, so you can later reclaim any items you may have added since your backup.

What's a clean System install and how do I do it? [9]

As a System Folder grows top-heavy with extra stuff, your System can become less stable. Sometimes parts of the System files get damaged or corrupted and you don't know

---

exactly which ones this happens to. Many times, Apple, software vendors, or Tekserve will insist that any problem you are having with your computer is due to all the junk in your System Folder, and will suggest that you do "a clean System install." That means making a brand new System Folder just like Apple would put on a new computer. This new folder will be lacking all your added fonts, custom doodads, and preferences (including your Internet access setup), so after you solve your problem you'll need to "dirty" the new System Folder again and hope that your problem stays gone. Some people try a much simpler dirty install first, which basically means deleting only your Finder, System, and Finder Prefs files and then running the System installer.

With recent G3s and G4s, you can boot from your Apple System Restore CD and either replace just the System Folder, "restore in place" (which will leave most of your Applications and user files and documents alone), or restore the drive to the condition it shipped from Apple, erasing all of your files and everything. (Multi-disc installers can only restore the entire drive, wiping everything on it.) Note that as with a clean install, all of these options will delete your Internet access settings and some or all of your program and other preferences.

For System 7.6 and newer, use the Options button in the main installer window to bring up the choice of a clean install. Your old System Folder will be renamed "Previous System Folder" and the new one will be called just "System Folder." (For Systems before 7.6, download an older version of this FAQ from Tekserve.com.)

Now restart to see if your problem is solved. If everything is okay, you can start "dirtying" your new System with all your old fonts, preferences, control panels, and extensions. It is always better to reinstall stuff like fax software from the original disks rather than using the old versions. However, you will want to move over any fax folders and preferences that contain your address books, old faxes, and so on. You'll also want to move folders such as *Claris* and *Aldus* that various programs may have placed in your System Folder.

We suggest doing this very slowly: move a few items, restart and see if things are okay, move a few more, and so on. This is a great time to do housecleaning—anything you don't want or don't recognize can be moved into a holding folder until you are sure you don't need it. The point is that anything that was freshly installed by the System install should not be replaced. Move only unique stuff that you know you need from the old System Folder to the new one. Remember that less is more. More speed, more reliability, more peace of mind.

You can automate the clean install process with Conflict Catcher or Clean-Install Assistant if you like.

What system should I use on older Macs? [9 & X]

If you have a PowerPC with a 233 MHz or faster processor and at least 64 MBs of RAM, we suggest that you use Mac OS 8.6 (with less RAM or a slower processor, use System 8.1). With any G3 or any G4, use Mac OS 9.2 or the latest version of Mac OS X. For Mac OS X, we recommend at least 256 MB RAM, and more is better. Both of these systems are more stable and reliable than previous systems.

On even older Macs, if your system is stable and happy and you don't need any new features, stick with it.

Any problems upgrading to OS 9.x? [9]

Mac OS 9 does have a few compatibility issues, but the good news is that most applications that work with Mac OS 9 will work with Mac OS X as well.

OS 9 does require an update to Adobe Type Manager. (At the end of 2002, ATM 4.62 was still available free on Adobe's web site.) You will also need to update software for Global Village PC Card modems, and updates for Virex and Norton Utilities are required. Other things that need updates are Suitcase, Visioneer PaperPort, Office, Word and Excel 98, many HP inkjets, Tech Tool Pro, Conflict Catcher, Soft-Raid, and AppleWorks. Sadly, LaserWriters with built-in PostScript fax modems are no longer supported.

Mac OS X

What's different about Mac OS X?

Mac OS X offers improved stability and reliability (but frankly, OS 9.2 is pretty stable, too). Behind the scenes, it is a more "modern" operating system with some of the new features people have asked for, like protected memory and preemptive multitasking. Among other things, this means that if one program should crash, you won't have to restart the computer. Also, a program will not hog your entire system (while starting up or performing a complex calculation, for example). Mac OS X also has numerous changes to the user interface, making it easier to do certain tasks.

Mac OS X includes a subsystem called "Classic" that allows almost all your old programs to keep running fine. However, to take advantage of Mac OS X's new features, you may need to update to "native" versions of your software.Check with the software publisher or with *http://www.versiontracker. com/macosx* to see if there is a free or paid update available.

Should I upgrade to Mac OS X today?

If you are a cautious person and your computer is doing everything you want it to, perhaps not. If you enjoy new things and like the new interface, or just want to be *au courant*, then go for it. There are also some great applications such as iPhoto, iCal, and iDVD that require Mac OS X. If you have an older, slower computer, like a beige G3 or early PowerBook G3, or any older PowerBook, you may be happier sticking with OS 9 (or buying a new Mac). Even if you have a faster computer, you may want or need to add some RAM (memory). If you are doing specific demanding tasks with your computer, like intense audio or video editing, your decision will be made based on your exact configuration of software and hardware. For instance, Final Cut Pro 3 runs great in X. But if you have an analog capture card, check whether the X drivers have been released and if people are happy with them. Most graphics programs have been upgraded for Mac OS X and work better than in 9 (or at least as well). However, as of late 2002, QuarkXPress is still a holdout and ATM Deluxe is not available, but InDesign, Suitcase, and Font Reserve all have been updated and work well.

Just before a system upgrade is a perfect time to back up your whole computer, or at least your important files. And don't forget, any major system upgrade requires some time to make everything right and to get comfortable with new interfaces and commands, so don't upgrade in the middle of a big project or if you are already stressed out.

Can I switch back and forth between OS 9 and Mac OS X?

For all Macs sold before 2003, yes. Use the Startup Disk control panel or system preference setting (works even if both OS are on the same disk). If the two OSes are on different disks, you can choose a startup disk (or CD) by holding down Option at startup until you see the Startup Manager. Click the appropriate icon and then the right arrow icon. (Apple has announced that beginning in 2003 new Macs will no longer boot into OS 9, although they will continue to run Classic.)

How do I know if my application is "native" for Mac OS X? [X]

While you are running Mac OS X, you can tell if you application is native by looking at the Apple logo in the menu bar (don't open the menu, just look at the picture). If it is a solid color, it is native, and can take advantage of all the new features in Mac OS X. If it is rainbow-colored, it's running in Classic.

What's with all these folders? Can I get rid of them? [X]

To start up, Mac OS X requires several folders to be in special places. (This isn't anything new. In Mac OS 9 and before, the *Control Panels* folder needed to be inside your System Folder, for example, and wouldn't work if you put it anywhere else.)

In the default 10.2.x installation (current as of the end of 2002), Mac OS X expects the *Applications*, *Library*, *System*, and *Users* folders to be at the root of your hard disk. Under normal circumstances, Mac OS X won't let you rename or move these folders.

However, if you restart your Mac into OS 9 for some reason, you must be careful not to move or rename these folders. (You'll also see a folder called *automount* and several files: *etc*, *mach*, *mach.sym*, *mach_kernel*, and *var*. Don't move or rename them, either.)

If you do change these files accidentally, you'll probably need to reinstall Mac OS X to get it working again.

Where are my documents? [X]

If you started from a brand-new Mac OS X system, they are in the *Users* folder, in the folder with your name. From there, look in either the *Documents* or *Desktop* folder.

If you upgraded to Mac OS X, then your old documents are just where you left them.

(Here is a more complicated explanation: Mac OS X can easily handle more than one user per computer, so it puts each user's documents in his or her own folder.)

Where are my preferences? [X]

User preferences live in */Users/<username>/Library/Preferences/*. This is shorthand for the *Preferences* folder, in the *Library* folder, in your username's folder, in the *Users* folder. Note that every user has different preferences.

Why are there so many folders in the "Library" folder? [X]

Mac OS X's "Library" folder takes the place of OS 9's *Extensions*, *Control Panels*, *Fonts*, *Preferences*, *Startup Items*, etc. Some of these folders still exist inside the Library folder, others have been renamed (*Control Panels* is now known as *PreferencePanes*). Also, the Library has consolidated several folders that never had a place before, such as *Internet Plug-Ins*.

You may have noticed that there are *four* (or more) Library folders on each Mac OS X system. Each user has his own folder in the *Users* folder. There is a Library folder in the root of the hard disk that is shared for all users. This can be changed only by users marked as administrators. There is a third Library in */System/Library* for Apple's use. Apple's installers and updaters expect certain files to be there, and you should not change them. Finally, you may have a Library folder inside the "Network" icon, which (on specially configured networks) may store network-wide settings such as shared printers and fonts.

I put something on my Desktop, but another user can't find it. [X]

Mac OS X is a multiple-user system, so it organizes folders on the disk somewhat differently than in Mac OS 9. Every user of a computer has her own Home Folder, so all desktops, document folders, and preferences are kept separate. Mac OS X is pretty conservative about security, too, and prohibits you from seeing other users' files. See the later question about sharing documents with other users.

I saved a document on the desktop in a Classic application. Where did it go? [X]

The desktop is a folder, just like any other folder. In OS 9 and earlier, the Desktop Folder was located at the root of every volume. It was normally invisible (but showed up sometimes while browsing servers, for example).

In Mac OS X, the desktop is a visible folder in every user's Home Folder. That is the desktop you see from every Mac OS X application.

While using an older application in Classic, however, something odd happens. When you browse the desktop in an Open dialog, you see a combination of both Desktop Folders. But when you save a document, it saves into the old, OS 9 desktop folder. This can be confusing for many users (Mac OS X 10.2 and later are smarter and put the file on your Mac OS X desktop).

Mac OS X puts an alias to the startup disk's Mac OS 9 Desktop Folder on the Mac OS X desktop for you. However, if you have more than one partition, you may need to create aliases to see all the files that Classic thinks are on the desktop. To do this, open a Finder window, and click on the "Computer" icon. Then open each volume, and drag the Desktop Folder to your own desktop while pressing ⌘-Option.

How can I get my windows to behave like they did in OS 9? [X]

Say you have two Finder windows open at the same time: Folder 1 and Folder 2. While typing in your favorite word processor, you click on Folder 1. Folder 1's window comes to the front. In Mac OS 9, Folder 2's window also jumps forward. But in Mac OS X, it does not.

You can get "Classic Window Mode" in Mac OS X with the free utility ASM available from *http://www.asm.vercruesse.de*.

I can't mount any disk images/I can't move programs in the Applications folder/I am getting "–192" or "–108" errors. [X]

Your hard disk privileges (permissions) need to be repaired. In OS X 10.2, this is done from the First Aid portion of Disk Utility (in the *Utilities* folder, in the *Applications* folder). For OS X 10.1.5, Apple has a Repair Privileges Utility for this: *http://docs.info.apple.com/article.html?artnum=106900*.

My system keeps telling me "There is no application to open the document...." [X]

There are two likely reasons why this is happening. First, you may not actually have an application that can read that file. If someone sent you a PowerPoint slide show, but you never installed PowerPoint on your computer, then you won't be able to open the file. If you don't need or can't afford all the features of Microsoft Office, ThinkFree Office is an inexpensive program that can open most Microsoft Office files, but it has limitations. The other situation is that you do have the application, but your computer hasn't understood yet that document *XYZ* can be opened by it. Mac OS X figures out document associations in part by their filename extensions, which is the part of their name after the last period. For example, the file *readme.txt* has an extension of "txt". You can show extensions on your System by choosing Preferences from the Finder menu and checking "Always show file extensions."

If you have a missing or incorrect extension on one of your documents, your Mac may have trouble with it. You can try to fix or add the extension. (Likewise, if you change the extension of a working document, it may stop working.) Extensions are important not only on Mac OS X, but also if you send documents to Windows users.

Here are some common extensions:

Extension	Indicates
dmg	Disk Image
doc	Word
jpg	JPEG photo
mp3	MP3 music
pdf	Acrobat PDF
ppt, pps	PowerPoint
psd	Photoshop
qxd	Quark

Extension	Indicates
rtf	Rich Text Formatted
tif, tiff	TIFF photo
txt	Text
xls	Excel spreadsheet

When I double-click on my document, it opens in the wrong application. How can I change this? [X]

Click once on the document, and choose Get Info from the File menu. Choose "Open with Application" from the pop-up menu. Then you can choose your favorite application from the icons listed. If you would like to associate all similar documents with this application, click the "Change All..." button.

How come in Mac OS X my scanner doesn't work/Real-Audio doesn't play/images don't import/plug-in doesn't plug? [X]

You probably knew that applications had to be rewritten to take advantage of all the latest features of Mac OS X. Unfortunately, a rewritten, Mac OS X–native application will ignore a plug-in that has not also been rewritten for Mac OS X. You should search *http://www.versiontracker.com/macosx* to see if the plug-in has been updated. (Unfortunately, some software publishers charge for their upgrades.)

Mac OS X Passwords

How can I change my password? [X]

Use the System Preferences My Account (in OS X 10.2 and later) or Users (in 10.0 and 10.1).

How can I change someone else's password? [X]

Log on as a user with administrative privileges, and use the Accounts (10.2) or Users (10.1) pane of System Preferences.

If you are not an administrative user, then you shouldn't (and can't) change someone else's password.

What if I forgot my password? [X]

You can ask your computer's administrator to change it for you.

If you *are* the administrator, it's a bit more difficult. Insert the Mac OS X installer CD. Reboot your Mac, while holding down the "C" key. This starts from the CD. At the installer screen, look in the Installer menu, and choose Reset Password. Choose your hard disk, and create a new password for yourself. Then click Save, close the window, and restart (don't reinstall Mac OS X).

How do I log in as "root"? [X]

Mac OS X systems ship with a root user, but with the user disabled. On Unix systems, the "root" user is the all-powerful account that can read, change, and delete every file on a system. Unfortunately, that power also removes all the protections built into Mac OS X to keep you from making catastrophic mistakes.

Here's an example. From the Terminal program, the command rm *file* removes (i.e., deletes) a file or an empty folder. So rm fish.txt deletes the file named *fish.txt*, and rm fish.txt cow.rtf deletes two files. The rm program deletes the files immediately—there is no trash in Unix. rm -r *folder* recursively deletes all files from a folder, and then deletes the (now empty) folder. So rm -r animals/ deletes the folder named *animals* and all its contents.

But what if you made a typo, and put a space before the slash? rm -r animals / will remove the folder named *animals*, and *also* try to recursively delete every file and folder inside /. That single slash is shorthand for "this computer, and all disks." If you are a normal user, or even an administrative user, you won't have privileges for /, and the command will fail. But if you are root, your Mac will happily carry out your command, without even asking "Are you sure?" You are destined for a major recovery effort.

So instead of logging in as root, here are other possibilities:

1. Try to do the action as an administrative user. You may not initially have privileges to do something, but you may be permitted to *change* privileges on a particular file or folder. Choose Get Info and look at the Privileges section to find out.

2. Download the program Pseudo. This will allow you to temporarily make a single program run with root privileges. For example, it will allow BBEdit to open and write to any file on your system. Since it changes only the program you specify for the time that program is running, it is much safer than logging into the entire system as root.

3. On the command line, use the command sudo (superuser do). This command will ask for your user password, and run one command with root privileges. For example, sudo rm -r /Users/olduser will delete an old user's home folder and all his files. All the cautions listed earlier still apply, so be careful!

If you still feel the need to activate the root user on your system, you can do the following: open the *Applications* folder, then the *Utilities* folder. Launch NetInfo Manager. Click the padlock in the lower-left corner, and type your username password to authenticate. In the menus, choose Domain → Security → Enable Root User. Make up a (nontrivial) password for the root user, and click OK. Quit NetInfo Manager.

To log in as root, you must first change the Login Window options. Open System Preferences, and choose Login. Then click the Login Window tab. Finally, turn on the option to show Other User in the login window.

You can now log out, and log back in with the username root and the password you just chose. Remember that you should use this account only when nothing else works. For your everyday (and every week and every month) work, use your normal account.

Mac OS X Multiple Users

When I try to save a file someplace outside my Documents folder, I get a file error and can't save. What gives? [X]

Remember that Mac OS X is a multiuser operating system and you may not have permission to write files outside of your *Documents* folder. Some applications don't report permission errors properly and you may get a file error instead. If you are the only user of your computer but didn't set it up, someone who did might have added a nonadministrative user with limited permissions as the default user.

So how can I share a file with another user on the same Mac? [X]

To share a file, you can put it in one of two places. If you want others to read the file but not change it, move it to the *Public* folder inside your home folder. If you want others to be able to read and change the file, move it to */Users/Shared* (meaning the folder named *Shared* inside the folder named *Users* at the top of your hard disk).

How do I get rid of inactive users? [X]

First, you should delete the user from the system. You can do this in System Preferences, using the Accounts or Users pane. Recent versions of OS X save the user's home directory as a disk image in */Users/Deleted Users/*. Older versions (before 10.2) ask if you want to reassign the user's privileges to an administrator. You should probably choose yourself. Then you'll be able to manually remove (or archive) the old user's documents and home folder.

But what if there is no longer a user to delete but there are still incorrect privileges? You could log in as the root user, or use one of several utilities to change the permissions of those files. Author Sandee Cohen suggests an easier way: boot into OS 9 and then open the files and resave them. This also works for files that you try to trash but don't have permission to. Take them out of the trash, reboot in OS 9, and then trash them there. (Note that this only works with Macs sold in 2002 or earlier…newer ones may not boot into OS 9!)

Printers

I chose my printer in the Chooser, and it forgot my choice. [9]

The Chooser is counterintuitive, because you can use it to make several simultaneous choices (printer, network drives, etc.). As a result, it doesn't display what's chosen. Once you select a specific printer, it will remain chosen until you select a different printer (unless your backup battery is dead; see later). To confirm what printer is chosen, select Page Setup from the File menu—at the top of the window that's displayed, you'll see the name of your printer.

Early Epson Stylus printer software can cause the printer choice to be forgotten—update to a more recent version.

To choose a different laser printer (or other AppleTalk printer) click on the appropriate driver icon on the left side (such as LaserWriter or LaserWriter 8). Sometimes you have to scroll down to see the correct icon. The specific Laser-Writer that you chose shows up on the right side and is highlighted. If it's not highlighted, you need to click on the printer name on the right side to choose it. If you are using a LaserWriter 8 or newer, there will be a little printer icon in front of the printer's name to show that you already "Setup" for that printer. If not, after highlighting the printer, click the Setup or Create button to select options for that printer. Then close the Chooser with the close box in the upper-left corner.

If you have an HP LaserJet or other non-Apple networked laser printer, pick LaserWriter 8 on the left side and then highlight your printer on the right side.

How do I connect my LocalTalk printer to my USB Mac? Printers like the LaserWriter IINT, NTX, F, Personal Laser-Writer NT, NTR, 320, LaserWriter Pro 600, 4/600 PS, Select 360, Color StyleWriter 6500, or an HP LaserJet with "M" or "MP" in its name? [9 & X]

To connect these printers to a new Mac, you must use an Ethernet to LocalTalk Bridge:

1. The AsanteTalk Ethernet to LocalTalk Bridge includes everything you need to connect a LocalTalk printer to a new Mac. It works with existing drivers.
2. If the printer is already connected to a LocalTalk network, you can use Farallon's iPrint LT. The iPrint LT is similar to the AsanteTalk, except that it has a PhoneNet jack instead of a LocalTalk Din 8 jack. If your existing LocalTalk network has more than eight LocalTalk devices on it, you need a much more expensive bridge, and you are better off upgrading to Ethernet all around.

One gotcha: Mac OS 10.2 and later no longer support Post-script Level 1 printers—only Postscript 2 & 3. So your old LaserWriter II NTX and other Postscript Level 1 printers will NOT work from 10.2 at all.

When I try to print to my Epson printer, I get an error message that the printer is not responding. What's wrong? [9 & X]

When you turn on your Epson inkjet printer, it performs a self-test before it enters normal operation mode. If one of the components fails the startup test, the printer enters an error mode in which it will not respond to any commands from the computer. Normally it will indicate the error with a flashing light or an error light. The first things to check are whether the paper is properly seated in the sheet feeder, and whether there is ink in the ink cartridge. When the printer is ready, you should see a steady green light.

I just upgraded to Mac OS 8.6 or 9.x and I can't find my printer's icon in the Chooser. Where did the driver go? [9]

If you own a LaserWriter Select 300, a Personal LaserWriter 300, or a Personal LaserWriter LS, Apple doesn't include the driver for these models with the OS because they have decided not to provide support for these machines. In other words, these printers do work with OS 8.6 and 9, but Apple doesn't guarantee that future versions of the OS will be compatible with the driver. You may download the driver for this printer from Apple's web site. The driver is called "Laser-Writer LS/300." But read the USB question that follows to use these printers with a new Mac that lacks a serial port.

If you own a LaserWriter Select 310, a LaserWriter II SC, or a Personal LaserWriter SC, the driver for your printer is completely incompatible with recent Mac OS. You must either downgrade your OS or replace the printer. The SC models are incompatible with anything beyond Mac OS 7.6.1. The Select 310 is incompatible with anything beyond OS 8.1.

If you have a StyleWriter 2200 or 2400, use the StyleWriter 2500 icon. If you have a StyleWriter, StyleWriter II, or 1200, use the StyleWriter 1500 icon.

For most PostScript USB printers, such as the LexMark E310 or E312, you must install the manufacturer-supplied Printer Description File and then use Apple's Desktop Printer Utility to create a desktop printer icon. Then simply highlight the icon on the desktop and select Set Default Printer from the Printer menu.

Connecting Old Devices to New Macs

Where is the audio input jack on my new Mac? [9 & X]

Many recent Macs lack analog audio input jacks, but they made a comeback on some Macs introduced in 2002. If you need to feed analog audio into a Mac that lacks an analog input, you need a USB audio interface, like a Griffin iMic (which is not a microphone at all, but rather a line/mic level to USB adapter), or a more advanced interface like an Edirol UA-1A or Roland UA-3D. If you are serious about audio on the Mac, you will be looking at more sophisticated products, such as the Digidesign mBox or 001, or a FireWire audio interface, such as the Metric Halo products or DigiDesign 002.

Why won't my speakers plug into the Apple Speaker jack on my computer?

The Apple Speaker jack is a special micro jack that is only designed to connect Apple brand speakers (although Griffin has an adapter to connect other stuff to it). Non-Apple brand computer speakers plug into the regular audio out mini-jack on your computer, not the Speaker jack.

How do I connect my old ADB device to a new USB Mac? [9 & X]

A Griffin iMate adapter works well for most mice, keyboards, and other ADB devices, including many copy protection dongles. But for more complex devices like a Wacom tablet with a pressure-sensitive pen, we suggest buying a new USB version for best results.

SCSI, FireWire, and USB

Macs don't come with SCSI drives anymore—do I still have to worry about this stuff? [9 & X]

Ultra-ATA (also called EIDE or IDE) drives have improved dramatically in the last five years, and performance differences between ATA and SCSI are much smaller than they used to be. But the price differences are still quite large. These days, we recommend SCSI drives (or disk arrays) only for certain audio, video, and server applications with very high data rates. If you don't have any SCSI peripherals and don't do multimedia, you don't have to worry about SCSI. If you do have SCSI devices, we can help you decide how to connect them (or replace them) when you buy a new Mac. For much more information on SCSI, you can check old versions of the Tekserve FAQ at *http://www.Tekserve.com*.

If my computer has both USB and FireWire, which type of external drive or CD burner should I get? [9 & X]

FireWire is much faster and is the preferred interface for these devices. Some hard drives and CD burners come with both interfaces, so you can use them with older computers that might lack FireWire. There are new versions of FireWire and USB in the pipeline, and USB2 seems to match some of the features of the current FireWire, but we still think that FireWire is a superior interface, even compared to USB2.

When I add a new device to my computer, like a USB Zip drive, should I install the software that came with it? [9 & X]

As Apple has upgraded the OS, they have included support for all sorts of devices. For instance, Mac OS 8.6, 9.x, and X already include drivers for most Iomega Zip and Jaz drives. In fact, the software in the box with the drive is probably old and out-of-date, and might even be incompatible with your OS. So we suggest trying the device first. If it works without installing new software, you are ahead of the game. And if you are on the Internet and plug in a new USB device that is not supported, the OS may offer to find the latest driver and download it for you. You can also check *http://www. versiontracker.com* for the latest driver updates.

Do I need special software or extensions to use FireWire devices? [9 & X]

Mac OS 9.1 and later versions, including Mac OS X, include basic FireWire device support and work well with most FireWire hard drives and cameras with no third party software or extensions installed. Some drives may offer slightly improved performance if you use the manufacturer-supplied drivers. But usually less is more, so try it without the special drivers first. For scanners and some other devices, you typically need to install the drivers that came with the device but check for updated drivers on the manufacturer's web site or *http://www.versiontracker.com* first.

Can I add FireWire or USB to an older Mac? [9 & X]

For desktop Macs that have PCI slots, you can add a FireWire or USB PCI card, or a single card that has both kinds of ports. For the PowerBook G3 Series, you can add a USB or FireWire PCMCIA card (or both). We recommend using Mac OS 9.1 or later if you install one of these cards.

If FireWire runs at 400 Mb/s, is it faster than Ultra320 SCSI running at 320 MB/s? [9 & X]

No. Did you notice that Ultra320 SCSI has a capital "B" (as in MB/s) and FireWire has a small "b" (as in Mb/s)? Ultra320 SCSI runs at 320 *megabytes* per second. A byte is 8 bits. FireWire runs at 400 *megabits* per second. To convert from bits to bytes, divide by 8, so FireWire is only 50 MB/s. It is still faster than any single hard drive can perform, and much simpler to configure. (Yes, you figured it out—12 Mb/s USB could also be called 1.5 MB/s USB.)

Is USB 2.0 better than FireWire?

We think that FireWire is technically superior, and as of 2002, Apple had not included USB 2 in any Macs. A new version of FireWire is expected in late 2003 that will leapfrog USB 2.0. Nearly all USB 2.0 devices work fine with existing Mac USB 1.1 ports, but aren't nearly as fast as they would be if connected via USB 2.

Why do people say that FireWire drives aren't "native" FireWire? [9 & X]

Hard drives have interface cards on them to talk to the outside world. Most drives have Ultra-ATA interfaces. Some drives have SCSI or Fibre Channel interfaces. None of the drive manufacturers have shipped a drive with a FireWire interface yet. All the FireWire drives that are currently being sold are Ultra-ATA drives with a special ATA to FireWire adapter attached. In early 2001, "second generation" ATA-FireWire bridge chips started shipping, and they offer greatly improved performance. If they ever make native FireWire drives, performance may improve further.

Is a FireWire drive fast enough for Audio or Digital Video? [9 & X]

With the new "second generation" bridge chips that came out in 2001, the answer is usually yes. DigiDesign was always very picky about which hard drives they supported for audio, and they now offer their own FireWire hard drives. DV has a fixed data rate that should be easily accommodated by these drives. However, if you are capturing analog video through a CineWave, RTMac, Igniter, Digital Voodoo, AJA, or similar card, you will probably have to stripe several FireWire or SCSI drives to achieve the needed throughput. For serious analog video, you may need to stripe four or more Ultra160 or Ultra320 SCSI drives. For HD Video, you might need to stripe as many as 8 or 12 drives, with two channels of SCSI controllers. Ask us or your local repair shop to configure an appropriate array for you.

Can I really have 63 hard drives on a FireWire bus? [9 & X]

Well, that's the theory, and maybe you can have 63 devices, but Apple's FireWire version 2.4 and older limited you to no more than 11 individual hard drives connected to a single CPU by FireWire. Apple's more recent FireWire implementation now supports up to 16 devices on a single chain (no more than 16 FireWire cables from your CPU to last device), and 63 total. To get beyond 16 devices, you need a FireWire hub to divide up your FireWire chains.

What is FireWire Target Mode? [9 & X]

On most Macs with built-in FireWire, you can press the T key while starting up, and the computer should enter a special FireWire Target (or disk) mode, indicated by a FireWire icon floating around the screen. That computer will then act like an external FireWire hard drive, and if you connect it to another FireWire-equipped Macintosh, it should mount on the desktop like another drive. You can then copy data back and forth. In some cases, you can even run data recovery or repair programs on a drive this way if a computer won't boot. However, on some Macs, you can start to FireWire target mode only if there is a valid System Folder (8.6 or later) on the disk, so if the computer won't boot and the system is messed up, you might not be able to enter FireWire target mode.

Monitors/Displays

Every once in a while, the image on my monitor begins to vibrate or shake. After a few minutes it stops. Any idea what could be going on?

Check the position of your monitor—especially if it is near the wall of your kitchen. Author Sandee Cohen tells us that one of her staff had a monitor that would begin to vibrate every time she heated up her dinner in the microwave oven, which was on the other side of a very thick wall. Microwave ovens can generate electromagnetic disturbances that can

cause your monitor screen to vibrate or shake. Similar disturbances can happen near large power transformers, and in
basements that are over subway lines. In challenged locations, a flat-panel LCD display (which is much less suscepti-
ble to electromagnetic interference) might be the best choice.

*How do I connect my old Apple monitor to my new Mac?
[9 & X]*

For the first ten years, Apple used a DB-15 connector with
two rows of pins to connect external monitors. If you have
one of these monitors, there is a cheap Mac to VGA adapter
that converts to the industry standard VGA connector, which
has three rows of pins. New Macs have had VGA connectors
for several years now.

*How do I connect my new non-Apple monitor to my old
Mac? [9 & X]*

Most industry standard monitors use the VGA connector
with three rows of pins. That fits right into new Macs, but
for older Macs, there is an inexpensive MacPNP adapter.

*How come my new non-Apple flat panel won't attach to my
new Mac?*

If the monitor has an analog connection, it's VGA plug
should go right into your Mac. But if it has a DVI connector
for more stable digital connection, you may need a $35 DVI-
to-ADC adapter.

*Why won't my new Apple brand monitor attach to my old
Mac? [9 & X]*

In 2000, Apple introduced the unique Apple Display Connector (ADC) to connect any recent Apple brand monitor to
most recent Macs with a single plug and cable that includes
power, video, and USB signals. At first, these new Apple
monitors worked only with new Apple CPUs. But now there
are products like Apple's own DVI to ADC adapter and Dr.
Bott DVIator ($150), which allow you to connect an Apple

ADC display to an older computer. But there's a gotcha: the older computer must have a Digital Video Interface, also called DVI. Some early G4s had this connector (before ADC). And you can add a PCI card with a DVI connector to any Beige or Minitower G3 or G4. Macs with ADC connectors also have VGA connectors for industry standard monitors to attach—or more recently, DVI connectors, but we have ADC to VGA and DVI to VGA adapters.

Even though I added a video card, I'm told that I can't connect two new Apple ADC monitors to one Mac. Can that be true?

If your extra video card has a DVI connector, you can get a DVI-to-ADC adapter that allows you to connect a second ADC monitor. This also works to connect a second ADC monitor to a 2002 Power Mac Tower with a dual channel video card (the one with one ADC port and one DVI port).

Can you run down all the choices of CPU video support?

- Beige Macs: DB-15.
- Blue and White G3 Macs: VGA.
- First Graphite G4s: VGA.
- Next Graphite G4s: VGA & DVI.
- 2001 Graphite G4s & Cube: VGA & ADC.
- 2002 Graphite G4s: DVI & ADC (dual monitor support); VGA adapter available.
- PowerBook G3 & G4: VGA.
- PowerBook G4 DVI: DVI, comes with a DVI to VGA adapter cable.
- First iBooks: no video output.
- iBook (Dual USB), flat panel iMac G4: Mini-RGB, comes with a VGA adapter. Some iBooks also have optional TV out adapter.

What are the different video connectors Apple has used?

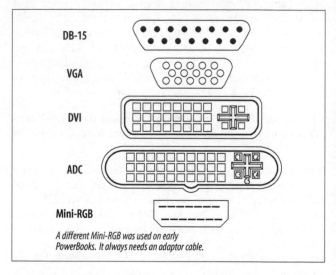

DB-15

VGA

DVI

ADC

Mini-RGB

*A different Mini-RGB was used on early
PowerBooks. It always needs an adaptor cable.*

Can you run down all the choices Apple of display video support?

- Beige Apple Displays: DB-15.
- Blue and White Apple Displays: VGA.
- Graphite Apple Displays: VGA.
- First Cinema Display: DVI.
- Current Apple Clear/Graphite Studio and Cinema Displays: ADC.
- Most non-Apple CRTs: VGA.
- Non-Apple Flat Panels: VGA and/or DVI.
- Barco and other high-end displays: individual BNC connectors (Mac or VGA to BNC cables are available).

My CRT has two faint grey horizontal lines across it. How do I fix that? [9 & X]

We call that the "Trinitron mark of quality." Aperture Grill CRTs like the Sony Trinitron and NEC/Mitsubishi Dia-mondTron have those internal support wires as part of their design.

Memory

I get "out of memory" errors in a certain program, even though I just added more memory to my computer. How do I get the program to know about the extra memory? [9]

Mac OS X eliminates this problem completely. But in OS 9.x and older, when you launch a program, it asks the system only for the amount of RAM set as its Preferred Size. You need to set the program in question to ask for more RAM. To do this, quit the program, and highlight the program icon. Then select Get Info from the File menu or type ⌘-I. At the bottom of the Info window, you should see a section called Memory Requirements. (With OS 8.5 and newer, select Show: Memory from the popup first.) Then increase the Preferred Size by 50 or 100%. If it says 4,096, try 8,000 (or 8,192 if you like base2).

Before increasing a program's preferred memory setting, it's a good idea to check "About this Mac" or "About this Computer" under the Apple menu in the Finder to check how much built-in memory you have. This will also show you how much memory is being used by the OS and other programs that are running. Don't set a single program to use more memory than is available. If you want to be able to run several programs at one time, be sure that the preferred memory of all the programs you will run simultaneously, plus the memory used by Mac OS, is less than the total built-in memory.

Please note that when running Classic applications under OS X, there is only 128 MB of RAM available to share among all

Classic programs that are running. You should really upgrade your memory-hungry programs to OS X versions.

What speed memory do I need for my particular Mac, and how much can I add? Should I add it in pairs?

This has become so complicated that we suggest you use one of the online references like MacTracker or call your local Macintosh Specialist. Before calling, please check your exact Macintosh model and write down the memory information shown in "About this Macintosh" or "About this Computer" under the Apple menu. You can get more detailed information about the memory in your computer with Apple System Profiler.

I just installed an Apple Firmware update, and some of my RAM has disappeared, or my Mac won't boot at all. What do I do?

In early 2001, Apple released a Firmware update for many G3s and G4s that disabled certain non-Apple brand memory. We think that in most cases there was nothing really wrong with that memory, but Apple was being very cautious. Your memory supplier should swap or upgrade that memory at no charge, or you can use the free DIMM First Aid program to update the memory yourself. But there's a gotcha—if all your memory is disabled, you can't boot the computer at all. So please run DIMM First Aid *before* you run the Apple Firmware update. We don't understand why Apple didn't include a test like DIMM First Aid in their Firmware updater itself.

Viruses

I think I have a virus. What should I do? [9 & X]

Buy the latest version of Virex or Norton AntiVirus for Macintosh. But don't stop there—the virus definitions that come with the product are probably already out-of-date. You must get the latest update for the program you bought. Updates are released online every month; new shrink-wrapped boxes are usually many months old. Install the program, update it, and run it. We've always had a preference for Virex, which you get as part of a .Mac account from Apple.

Powerbooks and iBooks

Does a battery drain when not in use? Are new batteries fully charged? [9 & X]

All batteries have some "self-discharge," usually 1% to 3% per day. That means that the battery will be dead after a month or two of sitting on the shelf and will need a full charge. Brand new batteries are always shipped without much charge, and must be charged before use. The Power-Book 500 series uses "intelligent" batteries that can get dumb if left uncharged for more than a month. This means that even if you don't use your PowerBook at all, you should plug it in for at least 24 hours every week so the batteries can charge. It's okay to leave your PowerBook plugged in all the time.

Is it okay to run my PowerBook or iBook without a battery? [9 & X]

PowerBooks have an internal rechargeable backup battery that saves your PRAM settings (printer, AppleTalk, clock, etc.). If you leave a PowerBook unplugged for a week or two without a regular battery installed, that internal battery will be depleted, your settings will be lost, and you may have trouble booting the computer. The regular battery also acts as like a ballast, maintaining smooth voltages to run your PowerBook. iBooks lack the internal backup battery and should always have a regular battery in place.

Should I get AppleCare for my portable?

PowerBooks and iBooks are manufactured more precisely, get rougher handling than desktop computers, and are expensive to fix. We think that Apple's own extended warranty program, called AppleCare, is a good investment for portables. Of course Apple is betting that you won't need it and that they'll come out ahead, but many of us would rather spend $249 or $349 on insurance to avoid the chance of a $500 or $1,000 repair. AppleCare doesn't cover broken plastic or physical damage from dropping or abuse, or service outside North America. AppleCare can be purchased only before your original warranty expires, and it cannot be renewed.

What's "resetting" the Power Manager mean, when should I do it, and how? [9 & X]

The Power Manager is software in the PowerBook that works to maximize battery life. It stores some special information for itself in the PRAM; if this information gets corrupted, you may have trouble running on batteries. When you have battery problems, it's frequently a real problem with the battery or the computer, but sometimes it's just a software problem with the Power Manager. Here's how to reset the Power Manager on different PowerBooks:

PowerBook 100

> Flip down the battery switch located on the back, and then press both the reset and interrupt buttons (on the left side) for 15 seconds.

PowerBook 140–180c (except 150)

> Unplug the AC Adapter, take out the battery, and leave it unplugged for five minutes. That's probably all you need for the 160–180c. On the 140, 145, and 170 (and just to be sure on the 160–180c), use two paper clips (or one paper clip bent into a U-shape) to hold in both the interrupt and reset buttons on the back for ten seconds.

PowerBook 150

> Disconnect the AC adapter, remove the battery, and use a paper clip to press the recessed reset button on the back for ten seconds. Then attach the AC adapter and press that recessed reset button momentarily—you will

hear a small pop from the speaker. Now use the regular power button to turn on the unit. Insert the battery and charge it for at least eight hours before trying to run on battery alone.

PowerBook Duo 200 Series
Remove the power and the battery, then press and hold the power/reset button on the back for 45 seconds.

PowerBook 500 Series
Press ⌘-Option-Control-Power On all at once. If the computer is on, it will go off (losing all unsaved work). If the computer is off, you won't notice anything, but you still have reset the Power Manager.

PowerBook 190, 1400, 2300, 2400, 3400, G3, and 5300
Shut down the PowerBook (Shut Down, not Restart). Then turn on the PowerBook and immediately press ⌘-Option-P-R. The Mac should chime once, the screen will go dark, and the green sleep light will be on. Now press the reset button on the rear. You may need to use the regular Power button to turn the machine on.

Original G3 Series PowerBooks
If the PowerBook is on, turn it off. Then use the key combo (Shift-Fn-Ctrl-Power on) that is printed on the back of the machine. Wait at least five seconds, then press the power button to restart.

G3 Series PowerBooks with bronze keyboard
If the PowerBook is on, turn it off. Press the reset button on the rear of the computer (find it between the video and modem jacks). Wait at least five seconds, then reconnect the AC adapter and press the power button to restart.

Original iBook and iBook (FireWire)
If the iBook is on, turn it off. Using a blunt object like a paperclip, press the reset button above the power button at the base of the display. Wait at least five seconds, then reconnect the AC adapter and press the power button to restart.

G4 PowerBook and iBook (Dual USB)

If it's on, turn it off. Press the reset button next to the video port on the back or side of the computer. Wait at least five seconds, then press the power button to restart.

NOTE

On the iBooks and PowerBook FireWire and G4, resetting the PRAM will also change the date and time setting of the computer, so you should check that after any PRAM reset.

Communications, Internet, and AirPort

Can lightning really damage my modem or Ethernet port? [9 & X]

Yes, whenever there is a big thunderstorm we see a number of Macs with dead modems come in for service the following days. We've also seen lightning through cable modems destroy Ethernet ports, requiring an expensive logic board repair. (One newspaper customer in the suburbs had the Ethernet destroyed on over 20 Macs during a storm; their insurance did cover it, but some policies exclude such damage.) We suspect it's more often people living in houses or brownstones with outside phone wiring rather than big apartment buildings, but we recommend unplugging from the phone line or cable modem during storms. Or you can try a surge protector with phone line or Ethernet port protection, but we haven't tested how well they work.

How do I save my Internet settings or switch among different service providers? [9 & X]

If you have OS 9 and earlier: Apple's TCP/IP and PPP control panels both have a "Configurations..." item under the file menu. Once you have your Internet configured as you like it, go to each of these control panels and export your current settings. You can also name and save configurations for several different Internet setups (one at home, one at the office, one on the road) and use the Configurations menu, control strip, or Apple's Location Manager to easily switch among them. Be sure to export all the configurations and save them on a backup.

If you have OS X: Make new "locations" in the pop-up menu at the top of the Network preference panel. This saves all your network preferences, TCP/IP, PPP, Modem, etc. Note that Mac OS X has an "all ports active" design and automatically switches to use an available connection (e.g., you unplug from Ethernet at work and go home, it detects your home AirPort network, and switches automatically). To disable this behavior, select Active Network Ports from the Show popup and uncheck the ports you want to be ignored.

How do I connect my Mac to DSL or a Cable Modem? [9 & X]

All recent Macs have a built-in RJ45 Ethernet port and will plug right in. The Ethernet port looks like a wider than normal telephone jack and may be labeled with a ‹···› symbol. Some older beige Macs have built-in Ethernet with both the RJ45 and an Apple AAUI connector. Use the RJ45. Even older Macs may only have the AAUI, in which case you need an AAUI to RJ45 adapter. Some Performa computers lack an Ethernet port, but one can be added in a PCI slot or Comm Slot (CS). You can also connect an AirPort Base Station to your DSL or cable modem and then use AirPort cards in any recent Mac. If you want to connect more than one Mac to a single DSL or cable modem without AirPort, you may need a router. For DSL, which uses Point to Point protocol over Ethernet (PPPoE), an AirPort base station or router has the added advantage of handling the PPPoE login and passwords, so your computer doesn't need special software to make the connection. When you have a router or AirPort Base Station, you'll typically set your Mac to obtain its TCP/IP address using DHCP.

Is DSL or a cable modem safe? [9 & X]

With DSL and cable modems, your computer is usually always connected to the Internet. Particularly if you have a fixed IP address, it becomes easier to hack into your computer. And with cable modems, other users in your neighborhood may be able to access your shared files or networked printers. (Look in your Chooser and Network browser to check whether you see anything that isn't in your own house.) You should turn off file sharing and web sharing, or at least set complex passwords. Depending on the importance and secrecy of your files, you may want to get a hardware or software firewall. An AirPort Base Station provides some firewall functions such as assigning random IP addresses, network address translation (NAT), etc. If you are not using AirPort, a router provides these services (and more) while allowing you to share a single cable or DSL connection among multiple computers.

Is AirPort really insecure? [9 & X]

Well, it's not the most secure network available. When your data is traveling on a wire, an intruder would have to tap it; definitely possible, but a bit of a hassle. With AirPort, your data is a radio transmission, still not totally in the clear, but a whole lot more available to the world. No encryption is really great encryption, and the WEP encryption offered by AirPort is considerably less secure than the SSL encryption in most web browsers. Recent studies have shown vulnerabilities in the security of IEEE 802.11b technologies such as AirPort and its WEP encryption. Keep in mind that using other encryption such as secure http (pages beginning with *https://*) and Secure Shell (SSH), to transfer sensitive information (credit card numbers, etc.) provides an extra layer of security, leaving pure gibberish in the hands of your friendly network intruder.

What about my AirPort Base Station? Can people steal my bandwidth? [9 & X]

First of all, set a decent network password. Don't use your dog's name. In addition, AirPort software v. 1.2 and higher

---

will allow you to restrict access to your base station based on the MAC address (or "AirPort ID") of the AirPort cards you have in your machines. You can find the unique 12-character AirPort ID on the label of each AirPort card or in the Apple System Profiler. Or, you may choose to share your broadband Internet connection with friends and neighbors.

File Sharing

I want to transfer files from one Mac to another. How do I do that? [9 & X]

There are many ways to move files from one computer to another: you can email them to yourself, burn them on CD or DVD, or copy them via Zip disks or an external drive (USB, FireWire, or SCSI, depending on your computers). In some cases, you might want a backup program like Retrospect to make a precise backup to tape or other media. You can also put files on an Apple iDisk or other network servers and then copy them back to the other computer. If both Macs have FireWire, you can use FireWire disk mode (press T while the computer is starting up) to make one computer act like an external FireWire drive that you then connect to the other computer.

Finally, you can network the two computers and use File Sharing to move files back and forth. This may be the best approach if you will be moving large files back and forth regularly. There are three steps: network the computers with wires or AirPort, share the files on one computer, and access the files from the other computer.

How do I physically network two or more computers? [9 & X]

If you are using AirPort or a DSL or cable modem router, the computers are already networked.

If there are two computers and nothing else, plug an Ethernet cable between the two. All current Macs autosense what they are connected to, so you don't need a special crossover cable (but a crossover cable works between *any* two Macs, even ones that don't autosense).

For more than two computers, use AirPort, a cable/DSL router with built-in Ethernet switch, or an Ethernet switch (available in sizes from 4-port to 48-port, which can be stacked for larger networks). Plug the Ethernet port of each computer into the Ethernet switch (or Ethernet hub).

How do I turn on file sharing? [9]

A shared computer is also sometimes called a *personal file server*. Although there are many steps, you only have to do them once.

1. In the Chooser (under the Apple menu), turn on Apple-Talk.

2. Open the AppleTalk Control Panel (in control panels under the Apple menu) and select AirPort or Ethernet as appropriate.

3. Open the File Sharing control panel. If you haven't entered an owner name, password, and Mac name, do so now. For example, use the owner name David, and the Mac's name "David's G4." Let's say the password is "backup2day." If you are on a corporate or school network or using a cable modem, be sure to use a serious password with a combination of letters and numbers, not "pass" or "please" or "chocolate." Passwords are case-sensitive.

4. Under File Sharing, press the Start button. If it says Stop, then file sharing is already on, so leave it alone. Close the File Sharing window by clicking in the close box. Don't worry about Program Linking—you can leave it off.

5. Now you have to decide who can access your Mac. If you are the only person to access this Mac, then you are done, and you can skip the rest of this question. If you never connect to a network outside your home, it's easiest to open the Users and Groups control panel, double-

click on Guest and click on "Allow guests to connect." If you are on a public or corporate network, using AirPort or a cable modem, or just paranoid, go to the File menu in Users and Groups and select New User. Name the new user and give him a password. When you are done, close the Users and Groups control panel.

6. Now you have to select what to share. If it's just you, or you and your loved ones, you probably want to share your entire hard drive. If you are on a network with many other Macs, you want to retain control, so you may want to make a new folder called "Shared" and only share that.

7. With OS 8.5 and later versions, click on the icon of your hard drive or the folder you want to share and highlight it. Select Get Info from the File Menu (or press ⌘-I). In the Info window, select Show: Sharing from the pop-up menu, and check the box "Share this item and its contents." You can then adjust privileges for any users you created.

   With OS 8.1 and older versions, click on the icon of your hard drive or the folder you want to share and highlight it. Go to the File menu and select "Sharing...", then check the top box "Share this item and its contents." You can then adjust privileges for any users you created.

That was a lot of work, but you only had to do it once. In the future, you can just use the File Sharing control panel (or the control strip) to turn sharing on and off.

Now that you've shared a computer, you can access it from any other computer connected to the same network.

How do I turn on File Sharing? [X]

1. Open System Preferences in the Apple Menu. Click on the Network icon.

2. In the Show: pop-up menu, select Built-in Ethernet or AirPort as appropriate.

3. Click on the AppleTalk tab, and choose Make Apple-Talk Active. Make sure you make AppleTalk active on only one interface at a time (Ethernet or AirPort, but not both).

4. Click on the Show All icon to see all the preference panes. Click on Sharing.

5. Under File Sharing, press the Start button. If it says Stop, then file sharing is already on, so leave it alone. Don't worry about the other types of sharing—you can leave them off.

6. Make sure that Computer Name is set to something that makes sense.

Under Mac OS X, you don't need to specifically set up sharing for folders. Guests can automatically access everything in the Public folder inside your user home folder. If you log in using your own name and password, you can access everything in your own home folder.

How do I access a shared computer over the network? [9]

1. In the Chooser (under the Apple menu), turn on Apple-Talk.

2. Open the AppleTalk Control Panel (in control panels under the Apple menu) and select AirPort or Ethernet as appropriate.

3. Open the Chooser under the Apple menu. On the left side should be several icons. Click on the one that says AppleShare.

4. On the right side you should see a window that says "Select a file server:"; if you have successfully shared and networked your computer, you'll see it listed there. Highlight the name of the shared computer and click OK.

5. If you took the trusting approach, click on Guest; otherwise enter the username and password that you previously set on the other computer. Then click OK. Next you'll see a list of the shared drives or folders on the

other computer (probably just one). Highlight the one you want and click OK. In a few seconds, the icon of that drive or folder should appear on your desktop. You can copy files to and from it as though it was another drive on your computer (but it will be much slower).

To avoid ever having to repeat steps 4 and 5, click on the icon of the shared volume and select Make Alias from the File menu. Next time you want to "mount" that shared volume on your Mac, just double-click on the alias.

How do I access a shared computer over the network? [X]

1. Open System Preferences from the Apple Menu, and click the Network icon.

2. Next to "Show:", click on the pop-up and select the appropriate port.

3. Click the AppleTalk tab and check "make AppleTalk Active." Leave the default to configure automatically.

4. Close the Network control panel, saving your settings, and return to the Finder (click the Mac face icon in the Dock).

5. Under the Go menu, select "Connect to Server."

6. After a couple of moments, you should see the name of the shared computer in the window that appears. If not (e.g., in an earlier version of Mac OS X), then look for the shared computer in "AppleTalk" or "*" or "Local."

7. Click on the shared computer name to highlight it and click the Connect button. (On older versions of Mac OS X, you might need to try looking under Appletalk.)

8. Enter the name and password you previously created on the other computer.

9. You will now see a list of available hard drives (probably just one). Choose one and click "OK." The shared disk or folder now shows up on your own desktop.

What if I followed the instructions above, and I don't see the other computer when I try to connect?[9 & X]

We assumed that your TCP/IP settings were already correct. If you have never configured TCP/IP (that would usually mean you don't have Internet access), then you might need to go to the TCP/IP control panel or Network preference pane and choose "Using DHCP Server" in the Configure pop-up menu. You might have to do this on one or both of the two computers. When connecting OS X Macs to OS 9 Macs, you might also need to enable File Sharing over TCP/IP in the OS9 Mac's File Sharing control panel.

What if I tried to follow these instructions and didn't find the control panels or choices I expected? [9]

You might not have all the file sharing items installed in the System on your computer, or you might have used an Extensions Manager to get some of them out of the way because you didn't need them. Find your System installer disks or CD-ROM, open the installer, select Custom Install or Add/Remove, and reinstall AppleShare, Open Transport and File Sharing. These are all found under the Network & Connectivity selection. On older Macs, reinstall AppleShare and File Sharing. Although you need System 7 or higher to enable file sharing, you can access a shared Mac from a computer running System 6—you just need to use the System 6 installer disk to install the AppleShare Client software on the System 6 Mac.

File sharing works well, but now my Mac is very slow to start up and takes an awfully long time to shut down after I tell it to. [9]

If file sharing is turned on, your Mac goes through an elaborate private ritual every time it boots up, checking the sharing status of every folder on your drive. When you shut down, your computer carefully unshares every folder on your drive before it completes the action. So, when you aren't using file sharing, turn it off. If you have a control strip, there is an icon for disabling file sharing. There's also an icon for AppleTalk. If you turn off AppleTalk, file sharing goes off too (unless you are using AppleTalk remote access). Apple-Talk uses extra battery power, so leave it off when you are "on the road" with your PowerBook.

Other Questions

I just bought a new Mac. Where is the manual? [9 & X]

New Macs come with a very short setup guide. The "manual" is under the help menu on the computer. If you are new to computers (or to Macs), or just want more printed information, you can buy one of many books that are available, such as *Mac OS 9: The Missing Manual* and *Mac OS X: The Missing Manual*, Second Edition, both by David Pogue (Pogue Press/O'Reilly & Associates).

How do I clean my screen?

Never spray anything onto the screen. Apple says to wet a lint-free cloth and use it to wipe the screen clean. Don't drip liquid down into the screen bezel. Don't use scratchy paper towels. "Kleer Screen" is the greatest. Apple and Sony both recommend it.

The clock on my computer keeps going back to 1904, or 1956 or something. [9 & X]

This means that the backup battery on your computer's logic board needs replacement. In most flat-shaped Macs and recent towers, it is pretty easy to do it yourself; in the Classic, IIci/cx, iMac, and beige tower Macs, you should let a professional do it. On a PowerBook, your internal PRAM battery may be dead—leave the PowerBook plugged in for two or three days to recharge it. After two or three years, a PowerBook may need its internal PRAM battery replaced by a technician. On both the iBook and PowerBook FireWire, some serious crashes (or pressing the reset button) cause the clock to reset. The crashing may be a sign of a problem, but the clock changing is normal.

Why can't I rename this disk? [9]

If file sharing is enabled, you won't be able to rename disks. Turn off file sharing. If this doesn't solve it, run Apple's Disk First Aid.

I got an error-XXX. What does it mean?

Frequently, your Mac goes through so many gyrations before it puts up the error message that the message may not be helpful at all. But shareware programs like System Errors, Apple Error Codes, or the Apple KnowledgeBase can help answer the question. For instance, –34 means your disk is full. Bus Error and Type 11 errors can mean almost anything.

How do I save a file on a disk that a Windows computer can read, or read a Windows disk on the Mac? [9 & X]

Mac OS 8.5 and newer have the File Exchange control panel (called PC Exchange in System 7.5 to 8.1). This allows the Finder to recognize and mount (and even format) DOS and Windows disks. For full compatibility, it's best to format interchange disks as PC disks on the Mac rather than on a PC. With System 7.1 and older, the Apple File Exchange program is included and will let you copy files to and from DOS floppy disks. Mac OS X inherently recognizes PC disks and has even adopted PC style filename extensions (which we thought we had escaped from).

To actually use Mac files on a PC or PC files on a Mac, you need a compatible application (like similar Mac and PC versions of FileMaker Pro or Excel) or else a file translator. Many Claris and Microsoft programs come with limited built-in translators, but MacLink Plus is a good universal translator. Microsoft Office files created on the Mac or PC are usually interchangeable with the same programs on the other platform, usually going forward or back one or two generations. However, newer versions may have features that are not supported in older versions, so simpler files are more likely to exchange without hassle. There are also several less expensive programs, such as ThinkFree Office, that can open Microsoft Office files.

You mentioned programs or updates I should have, how can I find them?

An excellent resource we've mentioned throughout this book is the web site *http://www.versiontracker.com*. This directory tries admirably to list every program available for the Mac, its most current version, and links to download any free updates.

There are separate sections of Mac OS X and "Mac OS" (OS9, Classic, and earlier). It even has a place for comments so you may know in advance if the update causes problems for other users. (Don't go crazy installing stuff you find there—less is sometimes more.)

Where can I donate my old computer?

Nearly any group accepting donations wants working computers, not junk. Many insist on fairly recent units that will get people smoothly onto the Internet. A few to try are:

http://www.cristina.org/dsf
http://www.thepencilbox.org
http://www.altschools.org/oace
http://www.sharetechnology.org
http://www.worldcomputerexchange.org

Isn't one service place as good as another?

Every service shop is only as good as their last repair. What we think sets Tekserve apart is that service is our business—our prime focus is on repair, upgrade, and custom configuration. We think that's reflected in our shop—no receptionist, no hidden service areas, just a bunch of well-equipped workbenches and technicians (and a huge inventory of parts).

We do sell lots of Macs and accessories, and in fact, we can frequently configure a system (or ten systems) and deliver the same day. Our approach to sales is based on service; not just trying to move boxes, but actually meeting the customer's needs. For instance, we offer turnkey Final Cut Pro video editing systems with everything you need to plug in and start editing. For corporate purchasers, we can configure and ship computers to multiple locations, with your standard software install already loaded and asset tags in place.

Our motto—copied from an old Walker Evans photo from the Library of Congress that we made into a postcard—is "Honest Weights, Square Dealings." And we mean it. If you are ever dissatisfied in any way with our service, please let us know and we'll try to make it right.

Do you really fix things, or just swap parts?

We've been humbled on this one. We started with the premise that we would always fix the broken part, not just swap it. But too many things came back with further problems and what seemed like a good policy backfired. People want their repair right now, but careful repair and testing takes time. So now we insist on swapping a bad part for a new or refurbished one.

So, yes, we actually fix things, but to complete the service quickly, we swap parts. We think it's the best of both worlds because it allows us to stand behind our work with a one-year warranty, and it reduces the need for people to use that warranty. (Our Apple warranty and AppleCare repairs are always performed with Apple Service Parts and carry a 90-day Apple warranty. Flat-panel LCD repairs and any repairs paid for by third parties also carry a 90-day warranty.)

Don't most other dealers swap brand new parts?

No. Service swap parts are guaranteed (although usually only for three months) to work the same as new ones, but Apple prohibits dealers from claiming that service parts are new. The parts are usually repaired and refurbished at Apple's depot.

Do you provide a messenger service to pick up and deliver stuff?

We prefer that you use your own messenger service, but in many cases, we can arrange to pick up and deliver (for an additional fee). If you send us stuff by messenger, please attach a note telling us who, what, when, where, and why. You'd be surprised at the mystery parcels we receive. We also deliver new systems, cables, and accessories by messenger, UPS, and FedEx.

What is Creative Solutions @ Tekserve?

Creative Solutions @ Tekserve, formerly called Smart Machines, offers complete solutions including design, implementation, and support for specialized systems that are used in video, film, audio, print and interactive production environments. Together with our technology partners, we are able to provide production-tested solutions that our customers can count on. Creative Solutions @ Tekserve is an Apple Value-Added Reseller and an Apple Professional Film Reseller.

Do you offer corporate accounts?

Our low-cost structure is geared toward payment by cash, check, or credit card when the service or purchase is completed. We are happy to accept corporate credit cards. We accept written purchase orders from Fortune 1000 companies, governmental entities, and most educational institutions. If your company's structure requires that you be billed and you have an excellent D&B rating, ask to talk to David and we'll send you a credit application.

Do you offer financing on new computers?

Yes, for individuals purchasing up to $20,000 of equipment, we offer the Apple Instant Loan program. For corporate purchases from $2,500 up to millions of dollars, we offer leasing plans from Apple Commercial Credit and others. All financing is subject to credit approval (and lots of other fine print).

Index

We'd like to hear your suggestions for improving our indexes. Send email to *index@oreilly.com*.

Learn from experts.
Find the answers you need.

Sign up for a **10-day free trial** to get **unlimited access** to all of the content on Safari, including Learning Paths, interactive tutorials, and curated playlists that draw from thousands of ebooks and training videos on a wide range of topics, including data, design, DevOps, management, business—and much more.

Start your free trial at:
oreilly.com/safari

(No credit card required.)